Volcano
Mount St. Helens
Before – During – After – May18,1980

Before May, 1980, Mount St. Helens in southwestern Washington State was considered to be one of the most beautiful mountains in the world. Its nearly perfect cone, however, indicated that it was a very young and active volcano. This picture was taken in January, 1980, from the mountain's north side, in an area that is now totally devastated.

Former height: 9,677 feet   Current height: 8,365 feet

Concept & Design: Robert D. Shangle
Photographers: Al Hayward, Doug Lorain, Robert Shangle,
Shangle Photographics and Virginia Swartzendruber

Published by American Products Company
Portland, Oregon 97202

Prime Distributor: United Products Corporation
2727 S. E. Raymond St., Portland, Oregon 97202
Phone: (503) 238-1166   Fax: (503) 238-0237

ISBN 1-884958-25-7

A small crater appears near the summit after the first minor eruption in late March, 1980. This eruption was the volcano's first since 1857, but gave little idea of the events to come.

The summit crater has grown larger and the entire peak is covered by a dusting of ash, after more minor eruptions in April and early May of 1980.

At 8:31 a.m. on May 18, 1980, the mountain exploded in a blast that was over 500-times greater than the bomb dropped on Hiroshima, Japan, during World War II. Here, the ominous specter of disaster looms above the small Washington village of Toutle.

The enormous ash cloud rises from the mountain on May 18, 1980, as seen from the west. This column rose to nearly 80,000 feet (15 miles above the Earth). The wind-driven cloud buried parts of eastern Washington, Idaho, and Montana under a layer of ash, and turned day into night as it blocked out the sun for many hours.

A view of the May 18, 1980, eruption from the south. The ash plume has begun to subside. The eruption lasted for about nine hours before temporarily dying down and laying the groundwork for additional violent eruptions later that summer.

Viewing the eruption from near Scappoose, Oregon, approximately 45 miles west from the mountain, on the afternoon of May 18, 1980. The eruption and ash cloud could be seen for hundreds of miles, and the noise from the initial blast was heard 225 miles away in Vancouver, British Columbia, Canada.

Viewing the late stages of the July 22, 1980, eruption as it appeared near sunset. This was one of several impressive eruptions that occurred during the summer of 1980. Thereafter, volcanic activity was confined mostly to growth of the crater's lava dome.

As seen from the edge of the devastated area above the South Fork of the Toutle River Canyon, west of the mountain. Notice the surviving forest on the right where the force of the blast (eruption), which went mainly to the north, was not felt.

The eruption's initial lateral blast produced a super heated current of gas, ash, and debris that travelled at hundreds of miles per hour. The heat and force of this blast destroyed some 200-square-miles of forests, leaving behind massive downed trees that look like match sticks, such as on the ridge shown here, a full ten miles from the volcano.

As seen with a full moon in July, 1980, a great gaping crater is left behind where once a lofty mountain stood. The eruption pulverized and ejected in the area of 1½-cubic-miles of material, leaving a massive hole in its wake.

Looking across the devastated area from above Mount Margaret, the once green landscape has turned grey, as ash, mud, and pyroclastic flow material covers the land. Sixty people were killed as a result of this devastating eruption.

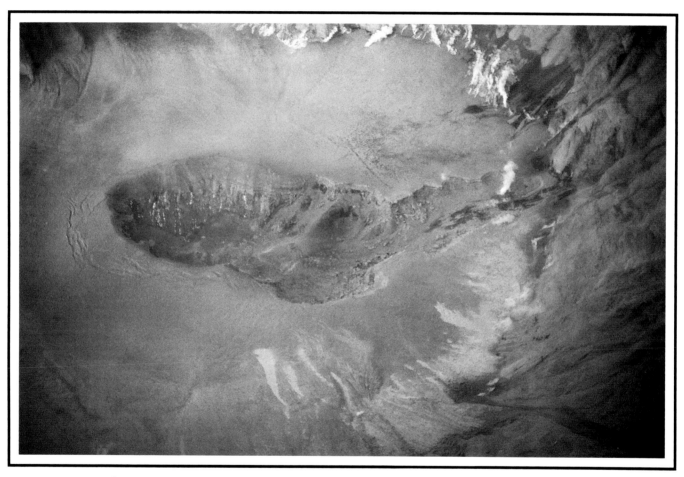

Molten lava glows inside the crater as the lava dome started to grow, in late July, 1980. The dome continued to grow, intermittently, for about six years. Scientists expect it to grow still larger in future lava eruptions.

The largest landslide in recorded history (triggered by an earthquake measuring 5.1 on the Richter Scale), along with mud and debris flows, composed of rock, ash, and melted glaciers, created this moonscape below the mountain. Mount Hood, another volcanic mountain 65 miles away to the south in Oregon, can be seen in the distance.

Winter snows cover the devastated area as ice flows form on Spirit Lake. Most of the area shown here is now protected as part of the 110,000-acre Mount St. Helens National Volcanic Monument, created by Congress in 1982. The monument is now a place of scientific research, recreation, and unique, stark scenery.

The first in a sequence of pictures viewing the mountain from across Yale Lake. This is the mountain's appearance in September, 1979, before the current volcanic activity began. (See the page opposite, and next to the last page in the book to complete the scenes).

Taken from the identical location as seen on the opposite page, this view shows the volcano in full eruption on May 18, 1980. The end results of this eruption, as seen from this same location, can be seen on the next to last page of this book.

Steam rises from the growing lava dome, as heat melts snow that has fallen into the crater. After several dome-building lava eruptions, the new 'mini-mountain' measured a height of 920 feet in 1996 and fills much of the crater floor.

A distant Mount Adams rises above the rim of Mount St. Helens and the steaming lava dome. Mount Adams is much older than Mount St. Helens and is classified as a dormant volcano, although scientists do not believe it is dead. The possibility of further eruption on Mount Adams cannot be ruled out.

Looking into the breach of the crater. Through this chasm enormous flows of mud, ash, and other material poured out at temperatures approaching 700°F. The flows raced down river valleys at over 60-miles-per hour and left behind incredible destruction.

Scientists still make regular visits to the lava dome and crater to record any changes in the landscape and to look for warning signs of future eruptions. Here a helicopter is dwarfed by the lava dome and crater walls.

The Coldwater Ridge Visitors Center is located along the reconstructed Toutle River Highway northwest of the mountain, as it looked in 1995. Note the jumbled remains of the large mud and debris flows in the valley below the mountain, still barren of most plant life.

Viewing the lava dome, Spirit Lake, and the devastated area as seen from the summit of Mount St. Helens, once again accessible to mountain climbers. Mount Rainier rises in the background – a reminder that it, too, is a volcano with the potential to cause destruction in the future.

Beargrass blooms on the relatively undisturbed southwest side of the mountain near Redrock Pass. Most of the eruption's force went to the north, leaving the lovely forests and meadows on the mountain's southern slopes intact.

A scene from above Norway Pass in the devastated area in 1994. A few flowers have taken hold and the ridges are beginning to grow green plants once more. Forests will eventually return to this area, providing a wealth of information to scientists on how nature recovers from such a catastrophe.

Viewing the shortened peak of Mount St. Helens, as seen from Mount Mitchell, south of the mountain. A full 1,300 feet of the former summit was exploded away, leaving the flat-topped version seen here.

As seen from Mount Margaret (north of the volcano) in 1994, the slow process of regrowth has begun, with low-growing plants and a few small trees that were partially protected from the blast by ridge lines and a heavy snow cover.

A full 15 years after the big eruption, logs, washed into Spirit Lake from the avalanche-created flood of May 18, 1980, still clog the lake, as seen here from below Norway Pass.

A harmless-looking puff of steam rises from the mountain. Reopened access roads and trails now lead to many viewpoints of the volcano, where visitors can see for themselves the results of the dramatic events in 1980.

This is a minor steam and ash eruption as seen in the Spring of 1981. For the time being, the mountain rests quietly. Scientists don't know when the next eruption will occur, but they warn that the eruptions of 1980 were not the volcano's first, and they won't be the last.

This picture completes a series of photographs taken from the same Yale Lake location as those shown in the center pages of the book. This is how the mountain looked in July, 1980, after the mountain erupted and the summit exploded into oblivion.

Young sightseers (not yet born when the devastation around them was created) visit the mountain near Coldwater Ridge, as the awesome power of nature is introduced to a new generation.